Mom and Me
A Day of Love and Fun

Bo Giles

Published in 2023
First published in the UK by THP Kidz Zone
An imprint of Tamarind Hill Press Limited
Newton Aycliffe, County Durham, DL5 6XP
Copyrights © THP Kidz Zone
All rights reserved

Written by Bo Giles

ISBN Hardcover: 978-1-915161-09-3
ISBN Paperback: 978-1-915161-25-3

Printed and manufactured by Lightning Source LLC

This book belongs to:

_____

It was a bright and sunny day, and Ellie and her mom, Maria, were excited to spend the day together.

Maria was a single mom, and Ellie loved having her mom all to herself.

Today was Mother's Day and they had lots of fun things planned.

They hugged each other tight, and Maria told Ellie how much she loved her.

"I love you too, Mom," Ellie said excitedly.

Then they sat down at the kitchen table to read a book together.

Ellie loved the stories her mom read, and Maria loved snuggling up with her daughter.

With all their reading done for the day, Maria and Ellie decided to bake.

They measured out the ingredients for cookies, mixed the dough, and cut out little shapes.

They'd wait for the cookies to be ready, and in the meantime, they'd find an activity that was entertaining.

"Remember our list," Ellie said. "It's time we make a tower with my building blocks."

Once the cookies were ready, Maria and Ellie sat down to enjoy them, each with a glass of milk.

They laughed and talked, and Maria felt grateful for her wonderful daughter.

Now it was time to do the cleaning up.

Maria and Ellie worked together to wash and dry the dishes. Even though it was a chore, they made it fun by singing together.

They finished the dishes and Ellie ran to her room. It was so she could get something she needed.

It was a bunch of flowers she'd bought with her allowance. She gave them to her mom, and Maria smiled and hugged her daughter, feeling grateful for the thoughtful gift.

They had more fun together, then it was time for bed.

Maria tucked Ellie in and read her a bedtime story.

She kissed her on the forehead and whispered, "I love you."

As Maria left the room, she felt proud of herself for being a great mom, and grateful for her amazing daughter.

They had a wonderful day together, and Maria knew there were many more to come.

THE END

www.ingramcontent.com/pod-product-compliance
Lightning Source LLC
Chambersburg PA
CBHW051323110526
44590CB00031B/4449